OUT OF *Africa*
& Into THE CLOUD

GIRLS CAN CODE TOO

DR. ISI IDEMUDIA

Your Curiosity at RESET 2021 will lead to a Great TECH Career.

Let's Smooth it!

Isi
2021

Paperback ISBN: 978-1-7347588-0-1

Publisher: Dr. Isi Idemudia

Creative Editor: Rising Above Publishing Services

Dedication

This book is dedicated to my daughters Ivana Idemudia and Shelomi Idemudia, who inspire me to be the mom they could be proud of. Who have watched me the last few years overcome some hardships but stood with me through it.

Also, to my Parents Dr. Innocent Masi and Mrs. Gladys Masi who have been my backbone through every phase of my life.

To my family, friends and followers, I do this for you all. Thank you so much for all your love and support you've shown me so far. I appreciate every word of wisdom, call, text, direct messages and repost. I love you.

To every girl who desires to grow a tech career, you are the reason I am pushing hard. I love you.

CONTENTS

ACKNOWLEDGMENTS

Annette Rippert - For lending her voice to my book by way of writing the forward and encouraging more girls to code.

Shareen Rivera - My Creative Editor for her simplicity and dedication that has made this final product possible.

Janine Cornecelli – For your dedication towards ensuring the forward gets presented the way it was.

Rep Kim Schofield - the Georgia State Representative for District 60, for her partnership in empowering more girls in Georgia District 60.

Mr. Bob Lax – Managing Director, Accenture Atlanta Innovation Hub, for his support in allowing me to give these girls, uninterrupted access to the Accenture Innovation Hub.

Mr. Chris Scott- my Managing Director, at Accenture who provided the opportunity for me to lead this initiative.

Mr. Chris Wegman- the Global Lead for Accenture-AWS Business Group, for his unwavering support.

Northcutt Elementary School- giving me access to their students for an hour of code 2018

Black Girls Code -for their partnership that has led to over 200 girls learning Artificial intelligence through this initiative.

Girls Who Code- allowing me to teach girls AWS cloud in the summer of 2019

Paul D West Middle School- for their reception and eagerness to learn more coding

Fulton High School- for stepping up to the occasion always.

Tri-cities School – for always answering the call to learn.

HYPE- for creating programmes that help girls learn to code.

Eastside Elementary- for the opportunity to teach Amazon Lex for an hour of code 2019

Dodgen Middle School- for the opportunity to be the Co-Chair of the Hour-of-Code Committee 2019.

APPRECIATION

My endless appreciation goes out to my friends who supported me financially during the production phase of this book.

Brepele & Ibiteme Danagogo
Raphael & Chioma Onoshakpor
Ofonime & Reagan Anusionwu
Oyenuga Oyebola
Micheal Ade Oraiade
Dr. Sophia Masi
Martha Okopi

WARDROBE PRODUCTION CREW

Special Thanks to this Production Crew.
Wardrobe: House of Julyet Peters IG: @julyetpeters
Ibiso Kejeh: IG: @lapis_bead_embroidery
Hair Stylist: John, IG: @kelechi_wigs
Makeup Artist: Busola, IG: @theglowzone_360
Photography: Kola Adetola, IG: @king_kola311

Annette Rippert

GROUP CHIEF EXECUTIVE –
ACCENTURE STRATEGY & CONSULTING

I first became aware of Dr. Isi Idemudia when she attended our Accenture AWS Summit on cloud technology at our Innovation Hub in Atlanta, Georgia. Isi was a very recent joiner – at the firm for just two weeks. I was immediately struck by Isi's enthusiasm and urgency as we talked about the potential and possibilities of cloud and tech careers. This enthusiasm can be found on every page of "Out of Africa and Into the Cloud," a biography and road map to overcoming obstacles and achieving your aspirations.

Throughout the book, Isi speaks for and to young girls and women who face obstacles and very real challenges in realizing their dreams of a career that may not meet their societal norms and expectations of a "female."

Isi's determination to find her way out of Nigeria and into a career in technology reminds all women of our roles in achieving collective success as technologists. Over the last two decades, we've seen enormous progress in the challenges tied to education, perception, traditional gender roles and cultural mentality. But there's still more to do.

We see many more women entering STEM programs now, and many organizations that Accenture partners with — like Girls Who Code and Code.org for Hour of Code — are having a huge impact on debunking myths and stereotypes about computer science education and career opportunities. "Into the Cloud" provides practical, applicable solutions that will help young women conquer remaining societal and personal barriers on the path to successful tech careers.

In 2018, Accenture published research called Cracking the Code. The results are still relevant and compelling today. We took a deep look at why we have such gender disparity in STEM. The findings were eye-opening. We discovered that girls and boys start out equally interested in STEM; but when they get into high school and college levels, the number of girls pursuing these subjects drops off significantly.

The reasons might surprise you. We found it wasn't a lack of interest. Girls still found these subjects intriguing. Instead, it was more around the lack of female teachers and female role models, plus a general sense of pressure by female peers that STEM just wasn't "cool."

I remember my own experience as a student at Northwestern. I was one of a handful of women in the engineering program, and it was a little daunting. And, as I moved into the corporate world, I likewise found a shortage of female mentors. I committed then to support other women in technical fields – women like Isi, who defy convention and incredible odds to succeed and continue to grow "technically" throughout their careers.

Isi and I both share a passion to teach girls to code and to empower more women in technology. I spent some time during Computer Science Week at an elementary school in Virginia teaching an Hour of Code to 5th graders. It was special to see the young girls in the class getting excited about coding. It is critical to continue to work with educational systems at all levels to nurture the next generation of women innovators.

Isi embodies this idea, sharing her experiences and knowledge beyond the classroom, encouraging women early in their careers to develop and expand specific tech skills for personal and professional success.

Each chapter explores a challenge and offers a solution, addressing the need to chase knowledge, become useful in times of adversity, embrace change and face our fears. These actions take courage, but there are people, like Isi, who will help girls, encourage them, support them in their journey.

Those girls, and all young women, are the beneficiaries of the courageous path of women just like Isi. They will be inspired, and, in time, they will inspire others, as we continue our journey as women together. I applaud Isi and recommend her book, which seeks to both enable and welcome the next generation of women coders, technologists and entrepreneurs to careers in computer science.

I'm a Nigerian woman and a coder, a rare combination. When I was working less than a year at Accenture, a leading global professional services company, I was contacted by a woman named Livia Chan, who was doing a series on women in the cloud. I was ecstatic but shocked that people were interested in my story, especially since I hadn't been with the firm that long. Even more shocking, was the continuous feedback that came in after my piece for their blog was published. People wanted to know more about my story and how I came from Africa into the cloud. I supposed I'm a bit desensitized to everything I've gone through to get to where I'm at, but reading the feedback from that article caused me to reflect on my journey.

Growing up in Nigeria, all I wanted to be was to do something that none of my peers were doing. If they were expected to go to college for certain types of degrees, I surely didn't want to settle for the society's expectations of me. After my high school at Federal Government Girls College run by the National Government of Nigeria, they used to be referred to as unity schools. I prepared for my Board exam in June/July 2000 (JAMB) and my standardized test (WAEC), both of which are widely used for college admissions. After successfully passing both exams in decent colors (not flying colors lol), I got accepted into the Rivers State University of Science and Technology to study computer engineering.

I never set out to study computers. I wanted to be an Architect at the University of Nigeria, Nsukka. Like many girls, I was conditioned by society to feel like computers were for guys. The thought of it sounded so foreign and difficult. By some stroke of luck, I didn't get admission into Nsukka for architecture but got admitted for my second choice at Rivers State University of Science and Technology (R.S.U.S.T) and I was accepted to study computer engineering due to my strong grades in mathematics, Advanced mathematics, physics and the sciences.

I started my bachelor's degree in pursuit in 2001 and graduated in October 2006. I learned coding sharing just 1 computer with 150 students in a grade level. We had limited time slots, so we would break up into groups to use the computer to run our little program. The rest of the learning was done by imagining if the code would actually run with errors or not.

According to a Women in Technology report by Accenture and Girls who code, there's a huge gender disparity between males and females in the university, where 52% of males take STEM-related courses, in contrast to only 30% of females. The gap is even bigger when it comes to the workforce, even though Women represent half of the U.S. workforce, but they hold just 25 percent of the jobs in technical or computing fields. What is more worrisome is that in 1995, 37% of computer scientists were women. Today, it's only 24%!

There are several reasons girls are less likely to study STEM subjects compared to boys, one of which is the notion that STEM is for boys, or STEM is too hard. I said all these things as a young college student. It's an absolutely normal and common way to feel because of the society we live in and the expectations placed on us as women.

Reflecting On my journey, I have also realized besides societal expectations, we females have certain hidden fears, which we hardly speak about, like the 'fear of the unknown', 'fear of rejection' from the technology world.

This book shows you how to overcome the hurdles as a woman in a male denominated field in a concise and easy to read manner. Focused on giving you the confidence you need to grow in the technology sector! This book is for females who suffer from fear of the unknown, lack of belief in themselves and lack of direction on how to be committed and thrive in the technology space.

I graduated in 2006 with a bachelor's degree in computer engineering and have worked in technology space for over a decade, topping it with a doctorate degree in technology management and working for Accenture- a leading global professional services company, providing a broad range of services in strategy and consulting, interactive, technology and operations, with digital capabilities across all of these services.

Alongside my career at Accenture, I have personally taught over 1000 girls in Greater Atlanta Area to code as my way of giving back to society. Females who fear that tech might not be right for them will derive the courage and the relevant tools to navigate successfully to a world-class career in technology.

I promise that after reading my journey to the cloud and following the extra resources I have provided in my conclusion, you would be confident in venturing into technology and knowing exactly how to smash it!

Don't be the person who procrastinates and talks about different technologies and tools and buzz words but never builds a career around it. Be the woman that others marvel at how they did it! Read along with me, let me show you how to build a strong technology career and be a formidable woman in the industry.

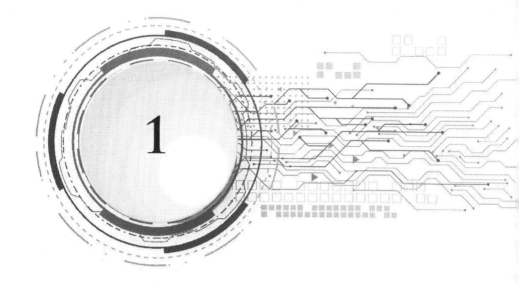

IN THE BEGINNING

*"I learned that courage was not the absence of fear,
but the triumph over it. The brave man is not he who does
not feel afraid, but he who conquers that fear."*

—Nelson Mandela

My first encounter with computers was in 2001 when I was in college at Rivers State University of Science and Technology studying computer engineering. You would imagine a college filled with computers in a lab, very sophisticated with glass doors and touch screens, but no, my computer lab had just one huge computer!

All the 150 students in the class and each user would access this huge computer via terminals. This was the case at Rivers State University of Science and Technology (R.S.U.S.T). We took turns to go to the single computer in the computer lab to copy C AND C ++ code we had written and stored on disk drives or quickly type out the code and pray that it executes without errors or at least minimal errors.

I remember a particular day in my second year when I took my first computer class. I had waited for my turn for an hour and then gave up. I was there thinking I chose the wrong field to study. Little did I know, computers were the future. I stumbled into studying computer engineering; I never set out to study computers. I had barely just heard the word by the time I gained admission.

My first year of College was not fun. I studied computers/coding from textbooks and lecturers' materials. I was frustrated thinking, how can I even touch and feel and smell this computer I presume to be studying?

EAGER AND ENTHUSIASTIC

In my first year of college, I took classes I thought were so unrelated to computer engineering like English, anthropology, and philosophy. I was confused initially because not only do I not get to work on or even see the computers, I now had to deal with non-science subjects and long theories and philosophies.

But by my second year, when I took classes like data structures and programming 101, I felt cool, like there was something I could brag about.

It was a new feeling—exciting and something to be proud of. When I was with my friends, I would always use these computer buzz words to show off my new knowledge. Even though I wasn't working directly on computers yet, it felt great to get my head wrapped around these concepts.

BOLD AS A LION

Hidden Fear, Embracing My Strength, Moving Forward

This is a topic I'm struggling to write, but I have to write it. I have this unsettling feeling when I dig deep into my fears. I was so scared when I saw my admission letter to study computer engineering. I imagined a class full of boys and boys in every corner of the engineering hallway. Yes, I was right. I walked down the hallway with guys staring at me like *what is she doing here*, and I even had the bold ones who walked up to me to ask if I was lost and if they might help me find my way. Truth is, I was afraid. I had secret fears I couldn't discuss with anyone, fears I muttered to myself every single day.

The society's expectation was that girls should be in the social sciences or art or not even go to college at all. Living in a developing country in Africa, the expectation was even worse than it is in the U.S. Below are some societal expectations and statistics of a typical girl from Nigeria in Africa. This will give you a picture of the odds against me.

With forced marriages of underage girls and female genital mutilation in the majority of the countries, it is a tough call being a girl in Africa. Human Rights Watch said that over 49 million girls are out of primary and secondary school in sub-Saharan Africa, with 31 million out of secondary education, undermining their rights and limiting their opportunities. Early marriage and teenage pregnancy are significant factors. In sub-Saharan Africa, 40 percent of girls marry before age 18, and African countries account for 15 of the 20 countries with the highest rates of child marriage globally.

Adolescent Pregnancies. The region also has the world's highest prevalence of adolescent pregnancies. In 14 sub-Saharan countries, between 30 and 51 percent of girls give birth before they are 18. Cultural or religious beliefs often stigmatize unmarried, pregnant girls, so that many pregnant girls are forced into early marriages.

"The African continent has one of the world's highest rates of adolescent pregnancy, but many governments insist on tackling this social and public health challenge by punishing girls and jeopardizing their future," said Elin Martínez, children's rights researcher at Human Rights

Watch. "Governments should focus on helping girls prevent unintended pregnancies and support their efforts to stay in school."

The girl child wasn't given much credit, but if you get up and stand out, the continent will recognize and applaud your effort. We have many girl children out of Africa affecting the continent and the world at large.

Amina Jane Mohammed is a Nigerian-British politician who is the Deputy Secretary-General of the United Nations.

Ngozi Okonjo-Iweala is an economist and international development expert. She sits on the Boards of Standard Chartered Bank, Twitter, Global Alliance for Vaccines and Immunization (GAVI), and the African Risk Capacity (ARC). Previously, Okonjo-Iweala spent a 25-year career at the World Bank as a development economist, scaling the ranks to the Number 2 position of Managing Director, Operations (2007-2011).

Chimamanda Ngozi Adichie is a Nigerian writer whose works range from novels to short stories to nonfiction. She was described in The Times Literary Supplement as "the most prominent" of a "procession of critically acclaimed young anglophone authors [who] is succeeding in attracting a new generation of readers to African literature".

Fear of the Unknown

Humans have always feared the unknown. Just like when Christopher Columbus sailed across the ocean, many people were frightened he would sail right off the end of the earth. There is always a stigma of the unknown for one main reason: we are not sure, and we do not understand the consequences. Psychology researchers suggest humans generally like to anticipate consequences. That's why the thought of failing at computer engineering was so frightening; I didn't know what to expect when I graduated. I feared the unknown. What was graduating going to be like? I had no role models in the tech space. I had no one to look up to who was a successful computer engineer or computer scientist.

My vision was blurred, and I wasn't sure I would even graduate. I came from a home where you couldn't even discuss dropping out; it wasn't an option. So I knew I had to finish and finish well. I thought to myself if I was in communications or journalism/media, there were so many females on TV I could relate to, or maybe music, dance, or art. I thought of changing fields at some point, but then I would be accepting the fears I had. In addition, I wanted to be an architect because my cousin had graduated from the University of Nigeria, Nsukka with a degree in architecture, and my dad (her uncle) wouldn't stop bragging about her. Aunty Vero (as we fondly called her) had since become a lecturer at the same university.

I could only achieve living life to its fullest potential when I had come face to face with the fear of the unknown. But as we all know, this is not an easy thing to do. It is a bit more complicated than just ignoring your fear of the unknown. I thought sometimes of just totally ignoring my fears and changing courses.

To conquer my fear of the unknown, I knew I had to be committed to making the changes within myself, and that is where it gets tough but doable.

Many sets of emotions are associated with fear of the unknown, and overcoming this fear requires you to dig deep to find the courage to actually step into the unknown. This is not what your fear of the unknown likes. All those deep-seated limiting beliefs will be resisting and fighting back because your actions will be challenging them and questioning their existence.

Overcoming Fear of the Unknown
Coming to terms with Your Fear

"Fear of the unknown... They are afraid of new ideas... They are loaded with prejudices, not based upon anything in reality, but based on... If something is new, I reject it immediately because it's frightening to me." What they do instead is just stay with the familiar. You know, to me, the most beautiful things in all the universe are the most mysterious." —Wayne Dyer

I realized fear is not unique to me, and everyone is feeling one form of fear or the other. Fear is part of our human DNA and so it is not unusual for me to feel fear when I stepped out into the unknown.

Funny enough, the human brain is hardwired to prefer severe negative consequences to uncertain outcomes. As long as the consequences, were "known," whether bad or good, the human brain feels comfortable. I knew I wanted to study something different—I landed into computer engineering by chance, as I said earlier. I didn't know what the outcome would be; I didn't have any females who had graduated with computer engineering or computer science degrees I could look up to.

But regardless of what the fear was, or what the reason behind the fear was, it made me settle in my heart that fear wasn't a 'me 'problem. It is an 'us' problem. The human brain does not like us stepping out into the unknown or living in a world of change.

1. Find the Bedrock of Your Fear

Then there is the fear that stops you in your tracks and stops you from living life to the fullest. This is the fear you need to understand why it exists within you.

The fear of the unknown comprises many thoughts and beliefs that result from negative past experiences. These are the beliefs that need to be identified.

My belief thought that:

- There can never be good and successful female computer engineers/scientists.
- I wasn't that smart, (remember I had said in Part A I couldn't get into architecture). The reason was that my English grades were not sufficient. This belief stemmed from this negative experience.

Negative experiences happen to everyone, even as little as tripping and falling in a meeting room full of guys, to have been part of a failed business or venture. These experiences usually lead to low self-belief, then your fear of the unknown will be heightened and wanting to protect you.

Whenever you face the opportunity to come out of your comfort zone and do something outside the "norm", spend some time analyzing the bedrock of your fear of the unknown. Once you have identified this bedrock, then you're halfway through the problem. Then next, you can brainstorm ways to overcome the hurdles you will come across.

2. Challenge Your Fear

We all know that our fears of the unknown are not based on reality because we fear things that have not happened. The fear of the unknown is based on our imagination of what might happen in the future based on negative past experiences. The future has not happened; it's still 'future', So this is where you take your fears to the alter and slaughter them as a lamb before the altar.

For example, I had to ask myself these questions:

1. Are there any female computer scientists who I knew couldn't get a job or start a tech company?

The answer was no, so I moved on to the next.

2. Are there any evidences I will fail, and my fear of the unknown will be right?

I truly didn't find any evidence that my fear of failure would be materialized. Yes, I had not made it into architecture, but I made it into computer engineering. Hmmm, I actually MADE it! If I made it, then I'm good at it.

After this slaughtering exercise, it really dawned on me that my fear of the unknown is not based on reality, so just challenge it and keep moving forward.

3. Riding the Wave of Fear

"Unknown is what it is. Accept that it's unknown and it's plain sailing. Everything is unknown-then you're ahead of the game. That's what it is. Right?"—John Lennon

---

Whenever we try new things in life that takes us out of our comfort zone, it comes with lots of discomforts, disruption, and feelings of uncertainty. This is absolutely normal and you will not be able to avoid the disruption of change in your life. There is a common saying that the only thing constant in life is change. However, once you accept that change is harmonious with life, the discomfort will subside, then riding that wave of fear becomes a lot easier. I spoke to a friend, Ibiso, who also studied computer engineering after she heard I was writing my memoir. She asked what exactly I was writing about. I told her I was writing about how I overcame my fears during my journey to the cloud. Her response got me smiling. She said, "Isi, I have known you right from college. We were classmates. You have never been afraid! You were jumping from school to NIIT to take classes, please, you have never had any fears." That was a confirmation that indeed, fear can be mastered.

All that fear—it's all an illusion.

A few ways I have achieved this:

- Talking to someone about your feelings is one good technique for managing your fear. I always talk to my twin sister, Chioma Masi, about all my bold decisions and the accompanying fears.
- Exercise, which helps me to relax and focus.
- Thankfulness helps me to slow my thoughts down and keep my mind focused on the present, not what may or may not happen in the future. I sing praises to God all the time.

- Giving back to society. Looking for ways to add value to people who cannot repay me helps me see there is more to life than my fears. To see that life is so much deeper. I find a homeless shelter, motherless babies, homes, or any volunteering opportunities to be part of.

4. Accepting Failure as an Option

Another underlying cause of our fear of the unknown is based on our fear of failure.

Nobody wants to fail, and it makes perfect sense, especially when we are about to embark on a new journey or path that will take us out of our comfort zone. If you really understand the bedrock of your fear of the unknown and have challenged your fear with these critical questions, then you just have to accept that failure could be an option.

"The guy who takes a chance, who walks the line between the known and unknown, who is unafraid of failure, will succeed."—Gordon Parks

---

If you cannot accept the possibility of failure is an option, then your fear of the unknown will convince you to stay put in your comfort zone. And, never take failures seriously, its just an event. It never ever defines who you are. Remember, your fear of the unknown prefers that you do nothing and live with regret than to step out and possibly fail.

If we consider that failure is actually a blessing in disguise, we wouldn't lose the idea of failure being experiences to draw lessons from. There will always inevitably be a positive outcome at some point through the failure in your journey. I remember failing Statistics 101, a second-year course in college. It was the only course I had an "F" for fail. I felt my world was going to end. It wasn't easy, it wasn't fun, and I had never had an "F" in my life before this. It was my chance to opt-out and go do something easy, but I went through the process of questioning why I failed, and once I had the answer, I set the course aside and continued with my other classes and NIIT as well. I retook that course in my 5th (final) year and made a "B". It was okay for me; I was already an Oracle Certified Proffessional, so it didn't matter.

> As said by Les Brown— *"The graveyard is the richest place on earth, because it is here that you will find all the hopes and dreams that were never fulfilled, the books that were never written, the songs that were never sung, the inventions that were never shared, the cures that were never discovered, all because someone was too afraid to take that first step, keep with the problem, or determined to carry out their dream."*

And as we go along in this book, you will see how I failed at several points in my journey and how I used that failure to my advantage.

5. Embracing Change

The one thing constant in our lives is change. We live in a world of constant and at times, disruptive change. The more we resist change, the more it will persist in our lives.

> *"By replacing fear of the unknown with curiosity, we open ourselves up to an infinite stream of possibility. We can let fear rule our lives or we can become childlike with curiosity, pushing our boundaries, leaping out of our comfort zones, and accepting what life puts before us."—Alan Watts*

Sometimes we confuse change with failure. Not every setback is a failure; sometimes it's time for the new to come in, but because we do not like to embrace change, we immediately classify it as a failure. It was easy for me to describe myself as a failure when I didn't get accepted to

University of Nsukka to study Architecture, but I took the other option, and I couldn't be happier for that decision. Today I look at my life, and imagine what a terrible building architect I would have been. If I didn't take or embrace that change, I wouldn't be writing this book today.

Fear of Nonacceptance

I feared the technology world would not accept me. It was a space for men; it was meant to be for my brother and my dad, not for me, I thought to myself. I wasn't sure I was going to fit in. I couldn't even talk when a guy was talking. In my culture, we were brought up that way. Girls don't speak when guys are speaking, so how was I going to even learn to code, when in my subconscious, this space was reserved for boys. I feared the boys would not accept me in class. If I had questions, who would I turn to? Who would be my buddy?

How I dealt with the fear of rejection.

- Identify what you really want.

According to Adam Sicinski, to overcome my fear of rejection or nonacceptance, I had to first identify what I wanted and why exactly I wanted those things. And not just mentally note it, but to write it down. There must be legitimate and compelling reasons for wanting to overcome your fear of rejection. Without this force or reasons, it will be wishful thinking and there will be little motivation to make a change. These are some of the questions I asked myself on a routine check and the responses I answered deep down in my heart.

- What do I want?
- What exactly do I want in life? What is my goal?

This should now give you enough information about your fear. And then next is to figure out what obstacles will be on the way. Think about the potential obstacles you might need to work through to overcome your fear of rejection. Ask yourself:

- What potential obstacles stand in my way?
- Itemize the obstacles.
- Are these obstacles real or imagined?
- Sitting in a quiet place to be sincere and honest with myself.
- How will I overcome these obstacles?

After analyzing my fear of rejection once I establish that it is a real obstacle in my way of success, my next instinct is to immediately reject it.

In the words of John Maxwell—
"Successful people reject rejection"—John Maxwell

Fear of Failure

In my head, computer engineering or science was hard; it was so difficult. Computers sounded so futuristic; it didn't make sense to many people. Truthfully, it didn't make sense to me. After I took other engineering classes like thermodynamics and civil structures, I would stay in my bed and cry. What was this? Is this what I signed up for? And these courses were not even electives; they were mandatory courses. In my head, it was hard, in my reality, it seemed harder. But I had no choice but to keep going. While I'm writing this chapter, the legendary basketball player Kobe Bryant, just died in a helicopter crash, and I cannot help but correlate the shared feeling we had on failure and resilience.

If you're afraid to fail, then you're probably going to fail
—Kobe Bryant

Doggedness

"I'm here. I'm not going anywhere. No matter what the injury—unless it's completely debilitating—I'm going to be the same player I've always been. I'll figure it out. I'll make some tweaks, some changes, but I'm still coming."—Kobe Bryant

---

THE BEAUTY OF PRESSURE

I always say pressure is a privilege. If pressure does not come, I feel insulted. Pressure makes me grow and achieve.

"Everything negative—pressure, challenges—is all an opportunity for me to rise."—Kobe Bryant

"I have self-doubt. I have insecurity. I have a fear of failure. I have nights when I show up at the arena and I'm like, 'My back hurts, my feet hurt, my knees hurt. I don't have it. I just want to chill.' We all have self-doubt. You don't deny it, but you also don't capitulate to it. You embrace it."—Kobe Bryant

---

CHAPTER SUMMARY

1. See failure as a detour that takes you to the same destination through another route.
2. We all have our fears, it's part of the DNA of humans. Never feel you are a rare case.
3. Success requires you to master that fear by confronting it: do that very thing you fear.
4. Don't confuse change with failure. When change comes, identify it for what it is and embrace it.—*Isi Idemudia*

BEING USEFUL IN
TIMES OF ADVERSITY

*"Anything that wouldn't make your future self
proud is a distraction."*

—Isi Idemudia

I had been in college barely a year and a half, and I faced the unthinkable word strike. Basically, it was a period where the university and the government of Nigeria could not reach an agreement on fees, taxes, salary increments, or bonuses, and the university would shut down and ask the students to stay home.

Yes, to stay at home, until the parties came to an agreement. Sometimes, this could be weeks, months, or years.

Growing up in high school, I had heard of the word strike from my uncles and aunts then going through the university system. I dreaded it because they would be bored and come to my house to wait out the period. My home was a five-bedroom house with two living areas on a 120,500 sq. ft (2.755 acres) house. Yes, it was a big house no doubt, but I have six siblings. So there's seven of us in the same house, with mom, dad, and nannies, and then all these uncles and aunts. It was not funny to behold.

So I am here to become idle and frustrated just like I had perceived my aunts and uncles. So I decided I would have to do something different with my time. I was so curious to know more about computers, to get my hands dirty.

RUNNING AFTER KNOWLEDGE

I shared my time between an IT training center called NIIT and college. During the strike periods, which lasted up to six months at some points. I refused to stay idle; I decided to learn and gain knowledge. Even if college was in session/open, I wouldn't have full access to a computer myself anyways.

I attended the Microsoft SQL classes for five months in 2002. This was the beginning of my hands-on interest in tech. In this class, I was focused on designing, building, and managing Microsoft databases. It was exciting to understand the concepts of database structures, how to create tables, and write queries.

I saw clearly that people were getting international certifications. It was a word I had never heard of. Being certified in the IT world was a stamp of approval from society. And guess what, it didn't matter if you were a girl or a boy as long as you sat for the exams and passed, voilà! You became globally recognized. I realized that certification had paths, to become a Microsoft Administrator, I would need to take a couple of exams, but each Microsoft exam I passed made me a Microsoft Professional. 90% of my class at college didn't know this. Nobody talked about it. Our lecturers never mentioned it.

The challenge though was that I was only able to take classes at NIIT Center when school was not in session. But it didn't deter me from being the best version of myself.

Self-Reliant

I continued to seek opportunities for learning and growth, and this better prepared me to compete for new or better opportunities in the workforce. Regardless of my career level, I never wanted to be in a place where I would become a financial burden to anyone. I never knew what the future held for me, but I knew with knowledge, I would be self-reliant. Even today, I never refrain from gaining more skills and abilities through continuing education because I believe I will be better prepared to provide the means necessary to sustain myself and my loved ones.

Going the extra mile to take classes at NIIT meant I could get a job, and by my final year in college, I was employed at NIIT to teach Oracle Administration. So I never looked for a job, in fact, I have never looked for a job for more than a few weeks. I have gone from jobs to jobs even in a country when the statistics of unemployment are super high. According to the Nigerian Bureau of Statistics, Nigeria's unemployment rate hits 33.5 percent by 2020. This is just to show how tough the situation is and was even in 2006 when I graduated from college.

I was always hot in the job market—in high demand. While my classmates got out of college and it took some two years to get a job, I was already working and earning a very decent living because I took the extra mile to seek knowledge.

TAKE IT WITH YOU

What I find fascinating is that the most satisfying reason to continue learning every day is that once I learned something, it was mine, forever! Nobody can lay a claim on it. Practically everything else in this world can be a lawsuit matter. Your brand-new car, your luxury items, houses, properties, all of these could be subject to claims. But learning something, it's mine forever. So I pursue knowledge every day by learning a new skill, reading a new book, attending a new class, getting a new certification, or discovering new truth. Every time I do, I will be able to discover who I am, become more confident and intentional, meet the challenges I face, understand those around me, and increase my knowledge forever.

"Knowledge is Power, Power provides Information; Information leads to Education, Education breeds Wisdom; Wisdom is Liberation. People are not liberated because of lack of knowledge."—Israelmore Ayivor

Paying Attention to my Environment

"The river of knowledge has no depth."—Chinonye J. Chidolue

I always paid attention to my journey. Even though I was taking SQL Server classes, I was paying attention to the trend and niche areas in my environment. There was a huge demand for Oracle Database Administrators, there was a huge e-banking boom in Nigeria at the time, and Oracle was doing quite a number of deployments and conversions. The NIIT Center was the number one stop for hiring managers. My father was very supportive when he saw my interest and the knowledge I was gaining. He offered to pay for more studies in NIIT. This was how I started my Oracle Database classes. Many commercial banks had sprung up in Nigeria and were heavy into e-banking, so there was a high demand for Oracle DBAs as this was a hot skill to have. Most banks were running on Oracle Financials, so that was the reason I turned to Oracle Database classes.

I would still be managing databases but on Oracle, not the Microsoft platform I started with. I was gradually becoming an authority in this field, at least far ahead of my colleagues.

"Focus on your focus."—Isi Idemudia

When I meet young girls, I always tell them to focus on their focus. And why it seems like it's a duplication of words or a repetition, it's just that we cannot overemphasize the importance of remaining focused. Based on my interactions with people doing the same thing I was doing at NIIT, I had an image of my inner self as a leader in technology.

Nothing would stop me, and I would stop at nothing until I achieved it. If a party would distract me, I would boycott it. If a friend would distract me, I would boycott such friendships. Nothing would stand in my way, not even my selfish desires.

---

*"Successful People Have Successful Habits.
Unsuccessful People Don't!"*

Some habits I formed were:

GOAL SETTING, SETTING A CLEAR GOAL.

I had set a goal that by the time I graduated from college, I would be an Oracle Certified Professional. This meant in 2006, I needed to sit and pass four tough exams

- Introduction to Oracle 9i: SQL
- Oracle 9i Database: Fundamentals I
- Oracle 9i Database: Fundamentals II
- Oracle 9i: Database Performance Tuning

This goal triggered my behavior. I had this clear in my head and this clear, compelling goal mobilized my focus towards actionable behavior. I used my goals to motivate me. If your goal doesn't motivate you, then it is not a goal.

"Whenever you want to achieve something, keep your eyes open, concentrate, and make sure you know exactly what it is you want. No one can hit their target with their eyes closed."—Paulo Coelho

---

Goals keep the Momentum Going

When I took my first Oracle certification, Introduction to Oracle 9i: SQL and succeeded, it was such an amazing feeling, I never felt such fulfillment in my life, until this point. This was in July of 2005.

Introduction to Oracle 9i: SQL Report Card

To become an Oracle Certified Associate, I needed to pass one more exam, the Database Fundamentals 1. I took both exams in a proctored environment in Nigeria with cameras and strict identification process. You had to pass these two exams to obtain your Oracle9i DBA OCA credential:

- Exam #1Z0-007 Introduction to Oracle9i: SQL
- Exam #1Z0-031 Oracle 9i Database: Fundamentals I

After mastering SQL in Oracle 9i, you needed to have knowledge of the Oracle 9i architectural components. This was very important when taking the second part of the OCA, which included Exam #1Z0-031 Oracle 9i Database: Fundamentals 1.

Seeing progress is so addictive. Like seriously, it's literally addictive because dopamine unleashed in my brain after attaining a reward. After a few months, I sat and passed my second Oracle exam! Exam #1Z0-031 Oracle 9i Database: Fundamentals 1.

Yo! I received an email from the VP of Education of Oracle all the way from Nigeria. I felt as if I was walking on water, flying a rocket to space. Just as a snowball grows in size as it's rolled down a hill, momentum works the same way. I was at the optimal state of mental performance.

Oracle9i Database: Fundamentals I
Examination Score Report

CANDIDATE: ISIOMA SANDRA MASI
PROMETRIC TESTING ID:
REGISTRATION NUMBER:
DATE: July 22, 2005
SITE NUMBER: NKJ
EXAM: Oracle9i Database: Fundamentals I
EXAM NUMBER: 031

PASSING SCORE: 44   YOUR SCORE: 58   GRADE: Pass

OCP HANDS-ON COURSE REQUIREMENT

Oracle Certification Program candidates who wish to obtain their Oracle OCP-level credential must attend one Oracle University instructor-led in-class or instructor-led online course from the list of approved courses located on the Certification web site at http://www.oracle.com/education/certification/ocp/index.here. Select the link for your OCP certification track; from the OCP Track webpage you may link to the hands-on course requirements. There is no course requirement for the OCA credential, or for OCPs upgrading from a prior version.

After attending the course, you will need to submit the OCP Hands-On Course Requirement Form.

Oracle OCP Hands On Course Requirement Form

ALL candidates for OCP-level certification must submit the Oracle OCP Hands-On Course Requirement Form.

- Candidates required to meet the Hands-On Course requirement should submit the form only AFTER they have attended their course.
- Candidates who are exempt from the course requirement because they took their first exam on or before September 1, 2002 may submit the form at any time.

For complete instructions on how to access and submit the form, go to http://www.oracle.com/education/certification/handsondo.html

Please accept our congratulations on your success. Feedback on your performance is printed below.

The following report lists the objectives for which you answered a question incorrectly in the Oracle9i Database: Fundamentals I test on the 03 scored items.

You may want to review and study the following objectives:

Within 30 days of passing all required exams, Prometric, Inc. will send your Oracle certificate by mail. If you do not receive your certificate, please contact fulfillment@prometric.com and provide your name, candidate ID, and current mailing address.

...examination was delivered at an Authorized Prometric Testing Center.

Oracle 9ifundamentals I Report Card

Goals Align Your Focus

My goal kept me in focus. I was halfway done, and I was in my fourth year of college. I had two more certifications to get. I became super busy; I was doing my internship at an oil and gas servicing company. There was the temptation to look into oil and gas, and by the way, my twin sister, Chioma, was studying petroleum engineering at that time. She has done her Masters in Oil and Gas Management and is doing her masters in the U.K. Goal setting helped me align my focus with my behavior because I always got feedback on my progress.

"Lack of direction, not lack of time, is the problem. We all have twenty-four hour days."—Zig Ziglar

"We are what we repeatedly do. Excellence, then, is not an act but a habit."—Will Durant

CHAPTER SUMMARY

- Let your goals be crystal clear, not fuzzy.
- The methods may change, but the end goal will always remain the same.
- Fall in love with the process of setting targets that help you achieve your goal and successfully smashing it. This way, you can keep repeating this process throughout your journey, as you will see in Chapter 4.

BURN THE MIDNIGHT OIL

Wealth, if you use it, comes to an end; learning, if you use it,
increases.

—Swahili proverb

There is an irony in life that still baffles me. But those that know it, exploit it to their advantage. The more I learned, the more it increased; it never finishes or diminishes. It is unlike wealth. If you keep using wealth, it reduces. But if you keep using learning, it increases. There were times I didn't quite understand all the topics taught. It wasn't always easy. Even today, I don't know every function or method in Python, a programming language I just picked up to learn by myself.

There are many times, it's confusing. Just know that you don't have to understand it all. Understanding a little is a good enough then be determined to learn more as you go along the way.

BUILDING AN ARMY

I built an army of people who had gone ahead of me and knew more than I did. I asked questions and set up study times to gain understanding.

In the moment of crisis, the wise build bridges, and the foolish build dams.—Nigerian proverb

As it is said in Nigeria, when there's a crisis, build bridges. I made tons of smart friends in NIIT from software engineers to database administrators, to those in the networking engineering side of the spectrum—all of whom are still in my network today.

And the areas I just didn't understand then, I knew it was okay. I couldn't know everything, and it was okay.

I celebrated that I sought to understand. That was enough for me. Technology is such a wide field with so many moving parts, catching up with everything was not a wise move. And looking back at those things I didn't know, right now I do know them. Some of these things just come as you keep moving along the same track. Never ever build a wall (dam) around you to prevent people from accessing you; you will never go far.

Wisdom is like fire. People take it from others.
—Hema (DRC) proverb

Watch your circle. The fire you catch is the fire you're close to. There cannot be a fire burning in Australia that will catch you living in Georgia. It's impossible. Choose the fire you catch deliberately.

My love for computers grew in leaps and bounds, and I just knew I wanted more. I desired more, I decided every evening I would spend my time getting more and becoming more. My God-given brain became a shared resource at this period of my life in 2003-2006, where I was taking Oracle classes at NIIT in the evenings after school and also taking classes in college during the day. I had observed at NIIT the hottest skills in the market—most companies, especially commercial banks, were trooping into the center to hire Oracle DBA skills. I told myself I needed to become an Oracle DBA.

I had two good friends (boys) in college in my class who were also students at NIIT. Both already had good programming jobs in college, working remotely and were making a lot of money while in school, and this was motivating. We started at NIIT at different times, but there is an African proverb that says:

> *Where there are experts, there will be no lack of learners.*
> *—Swahili Proverb.*

Both called Henry now lead their respective technology departments in Nigeria and the other in IBM Canada.

RECOGNITION

I began my journey as an Oracle Database Administrator DBA, taking classes on Tuesday and Thursdays from 5-7 p.m. I loved it; it was what was keeping me moving.

As I said in the previous chapter, I took the Oracle Fundamentals exam and succeeded, but it had not hit me yet what I was getting into. I had just scheduled my exam at the Prometric Center at NIIT and sat for the exam, I got a printout instantly, and I said okay. There was a verification craze; everyone at the center needed to prove their authority in their respective fields.

> *Learning expands great souls.—Namibian proverb*

There were so many great souls at the center in search of knowledge, and eager to learn. So many great souls, it was contagious.

Then I sat for the second exam at the same Prometric Center and passed. These two exams gave me the Oracle Certified Associate 9i title. I got the same exam result print out of my exam scores. These were the first times in my life I was getting my results of an exam instantly.

It was like magic. A few weeks later, I received a package from Oracle in the mail signed by the Vice President of Education. This was the game-changer. How could I sit in my little town in Nigeria in Africa and get global recognition? The letter read welcome to an elite group of professionals. Immediately, my perspective on life changed. Everything I had known about education and career had changed in just that moment. I could now add the Oracle logo to all of my credentials. Wow, all of my efforts began to make sense and pay off. So even though I was now in my third year of college, I was on global OCA—ha!

ORACLE

September 12, 2006

Isioma Sandra Modi

Dear Isioma Sandra Modi:

Congratulations on becoming an Oracle Database Administrator Certified Associate. By passing all of the tests in this certification track, you have joined an elite group of Oracle Certified Associates who have demonstrated a commitment to excellence using Oracle's leading technologies. Please note that if you are now half way to achieving your Oracle Certified Professional credential, so keep up the good work! DBA's are in high demand, so achieving your OCP will not only bring you great benefits from Oracle, but also increased job opportunities and higher pay.

Please note that if you are pursuing your DBA OCP credential, you must also complete at least one Oracle University hands-on course. You may view the courses that meet the hands-on requirement by visiting the OCA track web page. Visit http://www.oracle.com/education/certification.html and select the link for the DBA path you are pursuing. OAI, OAI and WDP students are waived from this requirement.

In recognition of your OCA accomplishment, we are proud to award you the enclosed Oracle Certified Associate certificate. We encourage you to display this as a symbol of your hard work and proof of your technical expertise. Feel free to include the OCA logo on your business card or resume for added credibility. You can access the OCA Members Site at http://www.oracle.com/education/oca. You will be required to use your OCA login and password to gain entry to the logo files. The login is OCA, and the password is OCTLOGO. Please do not share this information with those not certified as an OCA, as it will only tarnish the logo's equity in the marketplace if those who do not truly earn the right to use the logo begin to access it here. Please also take note of the logo usage guidelines.

Any future information will always be communicated to you through the email contact address you provided at the time of your exams. It is important that we remain in contact with you to keep you engaged with new happenings for the OCP community. Your email will never be shared or used for purposes outside the realm of Oracle Certification Program communications.

We hope you enjoy the rewards of certification. Please do not hesitate to contact your local Oracle University representative to plan additional training so that you can continue to stay on top of current and future technologies. When it is time to upgrade your skills using new Oracle technologies, be sure to take advantage of our one-stop OCP migration exams that will allow you to re-certify quickly.

For the latest information on Oracle University learning offerings and certification tracks, please visit http://www.oracle.com/education/certification.

Congratulations on your achievement and best wishes for your continued success.

Sincerely,

John E. Hall, Senior Vice President
Oracle Corporation

OCA Members Website
http://www.oracle.com/education/oca

Username: ▉
Password: ▉

Oracle Certified Associate (OCA) letter of recognition.

I wasn't playing on the same level as most of my classmates, I was part of an elite group of professionals. That's why in this world of information, your location is irrelevant to your success. Success is simply a decision backed with the corresponding action.

Oracle Certified Asscociate Certifcate.

THE FINISH LINE

Then I said I needed to get to the end of this Oracle journey. I prepared to become an Oracle Certified Professional (OCP), and that was the big one. It meant more recognition and more knowledge. I started studying more and more and spending a lot of time, even Saturdays, at the center. I then sat for two extra exams:

- Database Monitoring and Performance
- Database Fundamentals II.

A Congolese proverb says:

You do not teach the paths of the forest to an old gorilla.

Preparing and taking these exams became a walk in the park for me. Understanding the methods of the questions, how to time myself, and even what to expect. I knew the roads of the forest!

When I was ready to sit for my third exam, the shovel hit the road. The NIIT Center had issues with their Prometric server so they were not booking students for exams during the period I wanted to take it. The closest center was in another state—Warri Delta. This center was at least 200 miles from Port-Harcourt where I lived. The roads were not fantastic and bus fare to Warri in Delta wasn't cheap. I called them and booked my exam, paid my fees, and got set for my exam.

The exam was at 9 a.m., so I had to get on the 6 a.m. bus to arrive at 9 a.m. I woke up at 5 a.m. to get ready. Tired and worn out, I thought to myself, is it really worth it? Must I travel to sit for an exam? Seriously? Is this a mandatory exam? Of course, it wasn't mandatory. The world wasn't going to end if I didn't take the exam. My parents were already so pleased with my progress in school and the Oracle Certified Associate (OCA) designation I had received. But I had a goal set, and this goal guided my behavior and momentum.

Oracle 9i Fundamentals II Report Card

We all make excuses from time to time. Everyone is guilty of this. This is a simple habit we use to rationalize the "why," the reasons we didn't follow through on a specific commitment. If this becomes a norm and you've developed a bad habit where you make excuses all the time, then it might be time to curb this behavior and there should be no excuses why you shouldn't start today.

When I Lost All of My Excuses, I Found My Results:
—unknown.

WHEN I LOST ALL OF MY EXCUSES I FOUND MY RESULTS

There were a bunch of reasons I shouldn't have taken that exam.

1. The Exam center close to me was not scheduling, so I could've waited until they were ready.
2. I was a student, after all, I had achieved Oracle Certified Associate Level (OCA). This wasn't good enough.

3. The Exam center in Warri was too far, and I am not in the right mind frame to go that distance.
4. What if I had a road accident? Is this exam worth dying for?
5. What if I went missing in Warri? It is a strange area for me, and I have never been there? Is this not too risky?
6. What if I traveled for 200 miles and failed? What if this is the exam I actually fail?

"He that is good for making excuses is seldom good for anything else."—Benjamin Franklin

---

OVERCOMING EXCUSES

There are a few ways I have dealt with excuses. First, everyone gets excuses in their head. It's normal. Absolutely normal. The human body loves its comfort zone and will provide you several alternatives to prevent you from standing up and taking action.

1. Quit Comparing Yourself to Others

What you learn is what you die with.—African proverb

Why would you want to compare yourself with others, when everyone has a different appointment time to die? From the African proverb, everyone dies with what they learn. So we are all running different learning races. Just make sure to run your race with dignity and to the finish line. When you compare yourself to other people, especially those who think are achievers or have achieved what you want to achieve, you're focusing on your weaknesses rather than your strengths. And remember those people have their own weaknesses too. This will always make you feel defeated and hopeless if you see a big gap between where you are today and where they are or seem to be.

2. Quit Fearing the Unknown

George Addair is quoted as saying: *"Everything you've ever wanted is on the other side of fear."* People are wary of taking risks that could disrupt their reality and are often opposed to making even the smallest change to the comfort of their daily behaviors, even if their actions aren't in their best interest.

When you do the unknown long enough, over and over again, it becomes the known. By the time I had written these exams long enough, I was no longer scared to take any exam. I had made up my mind, if I failed, then I will take it again! Simple!

I went ahead and sat for the last exam, Oracle 9i Performance Tuning and smashed it!

3. Quit the Blame Game

One of the most destructive things you can do in life is to play the blame game. It is the basis for a large amount of frustration and unhappiness in people's lives.

The blame game simply put is blaming someone else for something that happened to you that was undesirable and staying convinced that it was someone else's fault instead of being proactive and making the necessary changes to resolve a situation. This often stems from irrational thinking and is not healthy for you or the person you are blaming.

I have had ups and downs in life, and I always take the blame, good or bad outcomes alike.

4. Be Deliberate

By crawling a child learns to stand.—African proverb

Be deliberate about your actions. Part of taking action is taking risks. You may have big plans that sound great in theory, but you never plan on actually following through with them. Stop making excuses and take deliberate actions that are necessary and in line to help you achieve the goals you want in life and create success for yourself. One of the first things you have to do to eliminate your excuses is to take that first step.

You learn how to cut down trees by cutting them down.
—Bateke proverb

5. Learn from Your Mistakes

By trying often, the monkey learns to jump from the tree.
—Buganda proverb

Not only can you learn what not to do when you make a mistake, but you can also analyze what went wrong and figure out how you can do better in the future. All mistakes are learning opportunities, no matter how big or small the mistake may be. Often, trial and error is the best way to work something out. When I failed, I always went back to prepare better and found a way to position myself for success.

6. Believing in Yourself

While I know you have heard this repeatedly, it cannot be over-emphasized. Whenever you face a challenge, a new computer science topic or subject for example, do you feel like you can handle it, or do you come up with some excuses to avoid it? Truth is most of us will come up with excuses. Because we doubt our own abilities to rise to the challenge and overcome the hardships that life throws our way. But whenever that self-doubt arises and we go ahead do the contrary of what fear expects of us, we WIN.

Fast forward to Late 2005, the NIIT center needed more instructors to teach Oracle, and I was invited and offered a job on a platter! I had no interview, the center Manager just said can you start the job tomorrow? Yes, my last year of college I was teaching at the center, making money and gaining more knowledge.

7. Visualizing Your Success

Literally, visualize what it would look like and feel like to achieve your goal and have success. Close your eyes and think about who will be waiting for you at the finish line and if there is no one, then imagine yourself at the finish line and the pride you will be feeling as you're running your final few meters.

Look at me, a small girl from Port-Harcourt, Nigeria with global recognition in my little hometown, a good-paying job, and yet still in college. I was living my best life and nothing would stop me! After all, I was an **Oracle Certified Professional.**

I graduated from College with a dual diploma, one from Rivers State University of Science and Technology and the other a diploma from NIIT center.

Oracle Certified Professional

CHAPTER SUMMARY

1. Never pray it was easy. The Challenges you face are actually setting you up for success.
2. Watch your circle, they must inspire you.

"If you look at the people in your circle and you don't get inspired, then you don't have a circle. You have a cage." —Nipsey Hussle

---

RE-ENGINEERING ADAPTABILITY

In 2017, I relocated to the United States. Events happened and I moved here to start a brand-new life and find better opportunities.

It was a brand-new environment, different culture, a different way of thinking. Once again in my life, I got scared. The thought of finding a way into the technology scene was overwhelming. I had no business contacts, and maybe my level of playing was too small for this type of environment.

One thing I did was not to put my head in the sand as though nothing had changed. Of course, a lot had changed; everything around me had changed. I anticipated the change even before I took my bags to get to America. Anticipating change helps you deal with the change when it comes.

But I knew to try stepping my foot into the river and getting on that boat and pedaling. Without pedaling, there would be no movement. No matter how expensive and pretty the boat is, it will remain still until it is pedaled. I registered my own IT consulting firm and built small applications and websites for a few high school friends who had moved to the U.S. right after high school. Then I said, "Hmm, maybe there's a thing here. Maybe there are opportunities for the level I was on."

Then I paid attention again to the buzz words in the USA tech scene, and especially in Georgia, because I had moved to Georgia to start a new life. I immediately started looking at how to become useful in my new environment. I saw that data analysis and big data was such a buzz word. I learned on my own using platforms like Coursera, EDX, Udacity, Udemy, and YouTube on how to analyze data sets. I learned a few tools, Microsoft Power BI and Tableau. Because I had worked with the database in Nigeria, data was an easy one for me to attack.

I never said, "Well I must be a Database Administrator in the U.S. because I was a Database Administrator in Nigeria." Things don't work that way. I just had to change and re-position myself for my new environment.

Embracing Change

Learning on the job can be daunting, but it is an experience that should be embraced. I took on small projects on Fiverr and Upwork as a freelance data analyst. I decided I would learn everything I could from my new environment to make my transition easier.

I took every project thrown at me. The ones I could do completely, I involved my friends and network I had made at NIIT. I had an ancillary of experts, from software engineers to graphic artists, to back end developers, just name it. I was committed to embracing everything that was thrown at me and to also keep a positive attitude to make the best impression possible.

I got a few gigs where I did data analysis and I volunteered at Georgia Tech—trying to make sense of the bulk of data a certain department was producing at the time. Yes, I worked for free. I got to their office, paid for my own parking, and made sure I got the U.S. experience I needed. I started applying for jobs, but no one would hire me because of too little experience in the U.S., so I kept doing this for a little while longer and to pay more attention. I heard LinkedIn was a big deal in the U.S. for job hunters, so I went on there and dusted my old profile, and started connecting with recruiters and seeing the type of jobs they were putting out there. Then I came across the term Amazon Web Services. I'm like what's that? It was everywhere and on everyone's lips. I had no money to take classes as I did in NIIT during my college years, and my dad would not pay for classes for me. By this time, I had almost completed my doctorate degree from the University of Port-Harcourt—I was left with only my final dissertation defense.

I embraced not only change in my career, I embraced the change.

Ask Questions

Even though I was doing small gigs, I really wanted to land big in corporate America. I never wanted to settle. If I was going to work, these were my top 7 companies:

Consulting Firms
Accenture
PWC
Deloitte
Products
Apple
Microsoft
Google Amazon *
IBM

Then I met someone on LinkedIn named Frank, who worked with IBM at the time. I had requested for him to recommend me for a role at IBM. He looked at my profile and told me you're not ready. Nobody will hire you with this profile! Aha!

I am never too shy about making corrections, especially from those who have gone ahead. I asked for help and he sent me a guideline on how to make a stunning LinkedIn profile. I did as advised in the guideline to portray my skills using keywords because that's how recruiters would find me.

After I did that, I set up some time on the phone where he reviewed my profile and still gave his input on it. I may write another book just on being seen on LinkedIn. Below are a few tips I used to get noticed on LinkedIn:

1. Keywords, Keywords, Keywords –

The most important key to being found on LinkedIn is keywords. The more keywords that appear in your profile, the higher you'll appear in search results.

*   So I asked myself, what are the words a recruiter might use to find people like me? These words are my keywords. I even have a section called keywords under my summary. So on my profile right now, you would find these keywords:

Keywords:
AWS | S3 | EC2 | ELB | AWS ARCHITECT|AWS CLOUD| CLOUD ARCHITECT|AMAZON WEB SERVICES|CLOUD | GLACIER | ROUTE TABLE | VPC | RDS | NOSQL | SQL DB | AURORA| DYNAMO DB | ELASTIC CACHE | ELASTIC IP | AUTO SCALE | AWS | ELB | CLOUD FORMATION | S3 | EC2 INSTANCE | LAMBDA | EFS | REDSHIFT | CLOUDWATCH | CLOUDTRAIL | KINESIS | ATHENA | CLOUD SEARCH | KINESIS| KINESIS VIDEO STREAMS | MEDIA STORE | MEDIA LIVE | MEDIA TAILOR | MEDIA CONVERT | BEAN STALK

- Use variations on your keywords such as "AWS" and "AWS cloud and "Amazon Web Services" - "Cloud architect" and "AWS cloud architect"

2. Headline –

Your headline is one of the most important 120 characters of your profile. This what appears on the search results in both LinkedIn and Google. Therefore, everything you learnt about keywords, should apply to your headline. *Use your keywords in your headline.*

- Include your phone and/or email address if there is room after your key words

3. Summary –

This is just like the summary of your resume. It should be clear and concise. It needs to eb able to explain who you are and how you can add value to an organization. It should be able to stand alone.

- As I mentioned above, use keywords and its variations in your summary as much as possible.
- Be forward thinking, let it describe more about what you can do now and in the future and less about the past

4. Experience (Work History) –

- Use a title someone is likely to search for, not necessarily the title you held.

If you seeking an AWS cloud role, go to google and search AWS Cloud jobs and find out that the top roles that show up are AWS Cloud Engineer, AWS cloud architect and AWS cloud Developer . While AWS Solutions architect sounds more fancy, it might not do you much good if your job hunting.

Then I got more views and emails from recruiters about different roles.

I have never been as afraid as I was at this point in my life, trying to break into corporate America.

A few things working against me here:

1. My accent was different
2. The U.S. accent was different, I could barely understand a thing.
3. I am a female.
4. I am a Black female.
5. I do not have a U.S. degree.

There's a reason I mentioned seven companies but listed eight and put an asterisk on Amazon. Follow me to the next section to see why.

Facing My Fears Again

Here I am again, 11 years later, facing all the fears I faced when I was in college. The same fear of the unknown, fear of failure, and fear of nonacceptance.

Only that at this point, the odds were more, and the risks were greater. I had two daughters to look after alone. So my success wasn't just for me alone, but it was for my children. I couldn't afford to fail. Failure was not an option.

These are a few ways; I addressed my fears: I simply answered these questions:

What do I want out of America?

➢ To be a thought leader in the technology scene.

Why is this so important to me?

> It is important because I want to be a mom that my two daughters would be proud of.

How will this benefit me?

> I will be able to pay my bills conveniently.

What will I lose if I don't overcome my fear?

> Lose my life and that of my daughters. Our lives depended on it.

This put my whole life into perspective. I had a good understanding of why I was afraid. Then I started to identify resourceful behaviors I could use to overcome this fear in optimal ways.

I asked and answered these questions that helped me identify the potential obstacles I had to work through to overcome my fears.

What potential obstacles stand in my way?

1. Accent
2. Color of my skin
3. Cultural difference
4. Social life

Are these obstacles real or imagined?

> Yes, they were real issues.

How will I overcome these obstacles?

> I would not change my color of skin, never, so what could I change?

Accent—I learned how to be understood by Americans. I learned that if I spoke slowly, they understood me. I am better at speaking English now, but there are still times I am not understood at meetings. I am not where I was when I arrived here, however.

I paid attention to American football because Americans love their sports. This was a good way to learn the culture. I believed once I was able to talk about their sports with them, I would be able to have conversations. Only in this country will you speak to a recruiter on Monday morning and they will use the first five minutes to talk about the game.

Adding Gas to My Tank

In my journey, I have found a few ways to boost my confidence when I feel it has been deflated. There are always times when we feel that way. Everyone feels it or has felt it at some point in their life. Below are some of the ways I added gas to my tank.

Find Something Familiar to Focus on That Keeps You Grounded

During my time of doing small gigs and working on my profile, I knew I had to update my certifications. It was now almost a decade since I got certified. I knew certification was familiar ground, so I sought the most relevant ones.

I only heard of Amazon as a retail e-commerce platform. To most people in the tech field in Nigeria at the time, that's what it was. When I got here, I noticed 4 out of 4 lined posts in technology I was following mentioned Amazon Web Services. I said to myself, what is this? I did my digging and discovered they were the leaders in the cloud. I said, cloud? What is the cloud? I did more digging and found out Microsoft also has a cloud component called Azure. I decided okay since I was already familiar with the Microsoft track, let me read and sit for the Azure certification.

After 2-3 months of study and hands-on lab in my apartment, I registered for my exam. I bought an exam bundle that included a retest in case I failed.

And yes, I failed my first Azure exam, AZ-3001. After a few weeks, I retook it and failed it again.

As I said in chapter three, I had many excuses at this point why I shouldn't pursue my career in technology anymore. Maybe I would have taken a job at Walmart, not that there's anything wrong with that, but that was not what I came to the US to do.

I was focused on learning from my mistakes and be better.

This was my first true failure. I was disappointed in myself. What was I going to tell my daughters? But I quickly got over it and never let it weigh me down.

Instead, I said:

There are several ways to catch a thief.—African Proverb

I decided to choose another cloud leader, and that's how I landed in AWS—yes, by **accident,** it wasn't by choice. Here are a few things I did to smash it.

- Third p arty training providers: : I read for it, watched $20 videos on Udemy, watched the videos repeatedly, practiced the hands-on labs, and got comfortable with it. If you are looking to get into technology , do not let lack of cash be a problem, there are so many free resources and there are cheap ones for the price of a burger, fries and some chicken nuggets. I used the course by Ryan Kroonenburg on preparing for AWS solutions architect associate exam. It was a great resource and I highly recommend Ryan's and acloudguru.com platform. There are lots of courses on there for you. The great thing is that they have other courses, not just AWS.
- Amazon web series training: I read the AWS frequently asked questions thoroughly. It provides great insights into the kind of questions others have asked. It broadened my horizon. AWS also has their free training on their website. I took advantage of that., so I could get into the mind of the exam provider.

- Practice questions: AWS provides some free practice questions. I used them to have a feel of how the real exams would look like. You can also search online for other practice exam providers if you have a few dollars to spend, but I didn't because I was broke.
- AWS free Tier account: AWS has a 12-month free tier deal for new customers, I signed up and used it for all my training and hands-on. You can surely take advantage of that.

After a few months of studying for my AWS Solutions Architect exam, with the self-help videos and hands on labs, I finally sat for the exam at a Pearson View center in KENNESAW on June 17, 2018, just as I did in Nigeria!

I'm like okay, this is familiar! Very familiar.

Take What is Familiar and Find a Way to Incorporate it Into Your New Routine or Environment

This quote from John Eliot:

"Confidence is not a guarantee of success, but a pattern of thinking that will improve your likelihood of success, a tenacious search for ways to make things work."

My confidence grew just by preparing and sitting for the AWS Solutions Architect Associate exam.

If something is familiar, we have clearly survived exposure to it, and our brain, recognizing this, steers us towards it. Therefore, perhaps we are hardwired to feel that the "known devil is better than the unknown angel."

I realized then that just like I made it in Nigeria, this was not any different. I could get all I wanted. Recognition, a great job, great life and any certification I wanted! It was all up to me to apply the same strategies I had used in Nigeria to set myself apart.

Embrace the unknown is only natural to fear what you do not know. This is part of human nature and is no reason to hide from the world or cower in the corner. If you truly want to settle into a new environment, you need to embrace the unknown as if it is an adventure you have no idea where it will lead you, but it is worth every minute spent on the ride there.

aws ✅ **CERTIFIED**

isioma idemudia

has successfully completed the AWS Certification
requirements and has achieved their:

AWS Certified Solutions Architect - Associate

Issue Date
Jun 18, 2018

Expiration Date
Jun 18, 2021

Maureen Lonergan
Maureen Lonergan
Director, Training and Certification

Validation Number V74LNRX1DM1Q15K8
Validate at: http://aws.amazon.com/verification

Amazon Web Services Certified Solutions Architect.

THE NEXT BIG THING:
ACCIDENTAL AWS ARCHITECT

I became AWS Certified Associate in July 2017 by accident, uploaded my certificate on LinkedIn, and with the strategies I learned from Frank, I attended 5-6 interviews but didn't get a job! But I was hopeful. At least interviews were coming!

Then I saw an AWS architect role at Accenture, and I had a contact who was a recruiter from Accenture in my network. Just as I had approached Frank, I approached the recruiter to recommend me for the role. She didn't respond. I gave it a few days and sent her another message on LinkedIn and got a response! It was all I was dreaming of! She sent me her email and asked me to send my resume to her. She wasn't the one recruiting for that role, but she would forward my details to the appropriate recruiter!

I sent her my resume immediately and the next day, I got an email from her introducing me to the recruiter Brooke Fairley!!

I had a chat with Brooke, after which she scheduled me for an hour-long interview with Hunter, this was one of the most difficult interviews of my life. Following that, I met with the MD of Accenture AWS Business Group, Chris Scott for half an hour. I received an offer all in 4 days!! Yes, I said it and you heard it, 4 days! I had an offer from Accenture, one of the world's largest IT consulting firms. What a dream come true, what confidence. This was my real breakthrough in Corporate America.

FEAR AGAIN

There I was, so very excited. I felt vindicated, working for one of the Big 5 consulting firms in the world—hundreds of thousands of hours of hard work poured into my hopes and dreams, and now I felt validated. But I also felt unfit for the job. I graduated from a university in Nigeria, how was I going to relate to people? When I'm asked which college I went to, how would I respond? In Nigeria, Accenture was and is a big name; it's a firm set aside for the smartest people in the block. It wasn't something I considered a normal girl like me would achieve.

I knew I would be working with some of the smartest people in the world, from all of the Ivy League schools I had heard of Harvard, Yale, Columbia, MIT. It was frightening.

I remember speaking to a friend, Will, who worked at Microsoft, and he said if Accenture hired you, then you can do it. It's Accenture; they knew what they saw. If they didn't think I could do it, they wouldn't have hired me, but they did. I felt I was underprepared for Accenture. I had panic chipping away at the edges of my thoughts whenever I thought about the fact that I started in a few weeks. Well, I went through the verification process, and there I was at my first-day orientation at Accenture.

COOL FACTS ABOUT THE CLOUD JOURNEY

The Late 1990s

In its early stages, the cloud was used to express the empty space between the end-user and the cloud provider. In 1997, Professor Ramnath Chellappa of Emory University defined Cloud Computing as the new "computing paradigm, where the boundaries of computing will be determined by economic rationale, rather than technical limits alone."

The Early 2000s

In 2002, Amazon introduced its web-based retail services. It was the first major business to think of using only 10% of their capacity. This was a major problem because companies were buying huge infrastructure but not utilizing it. The Cloud Computing Infrastructure Model gave companies the flexibility to use their computer's capacity much more efficiently. In 2006, Google launched the Google Docs services which were originally based on two separate products, Google Spreadsheets, and Writely.

In 2007, IBM, Google, and several universities joined forces to develop a server farm for research projects needing both fast processors and huge data sets. The year, 2007 was also the year when Netflix launched its streaming video service using the cloud and provided support for the practice of "binge-watching."

CHAPTER SUMMARY

1. When you fail, take it as a redirection, never the end of the journey.

2. As long as you see life as a marathon and not a sprint when things don't work out the way we want, we take another bend to the same goal.

3. Be flexible; change the methods but not the goal. My goal was to be an expert in the cloud!

4. Be inquisitive as a child, be eager to know

5. Go the extra mile when in a new and unfamiliar environment.

GIVING BACK

Wisdom is wealth!—African Proverb
Wisdom does not come overnight.—Somali proverb
He who learns, teaches.—Ethiopian proverb

In my day to day job as a consultant at Accenture, I do not just design cloud architectures for pharmaceutical companies, but for healthcare, hotels, airlines, insurance, financial services to mention a few. This multi-faceted capability enables me to understand the pain points of clients across different sectors. And to realize that though the requirements may be different in its specifics, the problems still come down to the same thing: efficiency, operations, ROI, and dealing with data.

Just like the growth of the cloud journey. I know my journey was filled with many unknowns. While I'm grateful for where I am now, it is my deepest desire to see other girls go through this journey with less drama than I did. So at work, I don't just do tech stuff helping clients do better with AWS cloud, I lead the community engagement team of AWS women in cloud initiative—an initiative set up by Ingi Zaki of Accenture Amazon Web Services Business Group to encourage more girls and women to join AABG. This has allowed me to impact 1000 girls in just 12 months!

In this completely voluntary role, I coach, mentor, and teach young girls what cloud is, what AWS cloud is, and building simple solutions using AWS services.

How I Am Inspiring Young Female Leaders

HOUR OF CODE 2018

In adapting to my new environment, I met someone who is the state representative for District 60, Rep. Kim Schofield, who has become a friend and buddy. I told her of my vision to teach the next generation how to code and the reasons behind my vision, which is my journey. In December 2018, I had informed Rep. Kim, that I would like to teach an hour of code at any school in her district. She was so thrilled and introduced me to the principal at Northcutt Elementary School. It was in honor of the hour of code, which is a campaign set aside by code.org as part of the Computer Science Education Week to teach millions of children across the globe to code.

Accenture has partnered with code.org for about six years at the time of writing, and it's a company-wide culture to use the Computer Science Education Week as an opportunity to give back to the world.

Rep. Kim Schofield and I have spent a few hours on the 9-11th of December 2018, at Northcutt Elementary School, where I taught about 100, 3rd-5th graders how to code. It was my first experience teaching U.S. kids. I taught them the concepts of AI and the methodology for building AI systems using Accenture's AI exploration tools.

GIRLS WHO CODE

During the summer of 2019, through Accenture's partnership with Girls Who Code, Accenture advocated for gender parity at work, with the Equal Together mantra and a vision of getting to 50/50 men and women at the workplace. As of writing, we have 45% women at Accenture and the leadership is working tirelessly to close the gap! The CEO of Accenture, Ms. Julie Sweet, is a woman! The first time ever a woman is in that seat.

I led an AWS Cloud session, where I taught 100 girls from Girls Who Code, a nonprofit organization set up to support and increase the number of women in computer science by equipping women with the necessary skills to pursue 21st-century skills.

In my session on June 3, 2019, I led a session teaching 100 girls how to code with Python using an AWS DynamoDB game called CodeCombat. In this game, they had to survive the jungle using Python commands. What a fun way to learn! I never learned that way, so what a privilege it was for me to teach that way.

GIRLS WHO CODE SUMMER IMMERSION PROGRAM 2019

BLACK GIRLS CODE

I also had the privilege to coach 100 girls from Black Girls Code during the same summer of 2019, on how to code using Python and to build an Alexa skill.

I remember having lunch with the representative and she asked me how our partnership could do more for her community. She is so passionate about District 60, she wants to see them better and do more. "Isi, how can you help my community of girls?" she asked.

She introduced me to Black Girls Code, an organization focused on increasing the number of women of color in the digital space by empowering girls of color ages 7 to 17 to become innovators in STEM fields. The date was fixed for July 18, 2019, and my daughters and I were set to travel to Tampa, Florida for our vacation on a night flight. If you live in Atlanta, you know the traffic, so I thought to myself, if I finished this coaching event at 4 p.m., making it back home to pick up my girls, then hitting the airport would be near impossible. So a friend at Accenture, who was part of the planning team of the event, told me, "Isi, why not bring your girls for the coding session? After all, your girls are Black and they can code." Voila!

It hit me hard. I had to bring my girls in the process to begin their journey too.

BLACK GRILS CODE SUMMER SHOWCASE AT THE ATLANTA INNOVATION HUB JULY 18, 2019

From left, Mr. Bob Lax, Isi Idemudia, Jonette Jones and Laura Segura at the black girls code summer showcase.

BLACK GIRLS CODE SUMMER SHOWCASE (Design thinking session) AT THE ATLANTA INNOVATION HUB JULY 18, 2019

BLACK GIRLS CODE SUMMER SHOWCASE AT THE ATLANTA INNOVATION HUB JULY 18, 2019

AWS CLOUD SESSION

GEORGIA DISTRICT 60
TECHNOLOGY FIELD TRIP

In December 2019, I worked with the State Representative Kim Schofield, to teach 100 girls how to build chatbots using Amazon Lex, how to build Alexa Skills, and Deep Racer.

The partnership with the state representative is particularly satisfying because I can reach a wider audience using her influence. In honor of the Computer Science Education Week, Representative Kim Schofield and I invited 100 high school female students from:

Forest Park High School
Tri-Cities School
Paul D. West Middle School
North Clayton Middle School

GA DISTRICT 60 FIELD TRIP DEC 9, 2019 AT THE ACCENTURE ATLANTA
INNOVATION HUB WITH REP. KIM SCHOFIELD AND MANAGING
DIRECTOR AT ACCENTURE HUB, MR. BOB LAX

My Inspiration

Dodgen Middle School

I am Blessed with two beautiful daughters, Ivana and Shelomi, and I make them feel worthy of themselves and feel it is okay to look the way they do.

In honor of the Computer Science Education Week, I volunteered at my daughter's school, Dodgen Middle School to teach 100 children how to code and, of course, my daughter Ivana, who is in 6th grade, registered for the classes. They were before school classes for those who indicated interest.

When I got the link in the school's newsletter, I quickly registered her and informed her.

She had such an amazing session building her first chatbots along with 75 other students over a three-day period, and this was super fulfilling seeing my own daughter code AI systems.

The Principal of the school, Dr. Alford, was at the three days sessions as well as the representative of the PTSA board, Ms. Donna.

East Side Elementary School

The last day of the 2019 Computer Science Education Week, Friday, December 15th, 2019. I was at my youngest daughter's class for an hour to teach them to build AI systems. I contacted her teacher (Ms. Campbell) at the beginning of the term and told her I would love to come in for an hour to do some coding. And she indulged.

My daughter, Shelomi, is in 5th grade, and what a delight to see her and 25 of her classmates build chatbots and learn about artificial intelligence.

From left, Isi Idemudia, Shelomi Idemudia (My Daugther), Ms. Bethany Campbell-5th Grade below after a successful hour of code.

CHAPTER SUMMARY

- Rivers don't drink their own waters; trees don't eat their own fruits. The salt seasons the soup in order to have its purpose fulfilled. Live for others! Israelmore Ayivor
- Always find opportunities to give back and help. Be a river!

Do not throw away the ladders that you used to climb to the top. Because you may need it on your way down. —African Proverb

---

LOOKING AHEAD

Female Technology Leaders

I have put together a shortlist of female technology leaders who I look up to, in no particular order. Growing up as a young girl, I didn't have any. I want you to have the opportunity to meet these great women of worth.

- Twanna Hayes, Chief technology officer, City of Atlanta

Annette Rippert

- Group Chief Executive—Accenture Strategy & Consulting

Robbin Jones, Sr. IT product leader, the Coca-Cola company

Kesha Williams is an Alexa Champion,
AWS Machine Learning Hero, and technical instructor
with A Cloud Guru

Ginni Rometty—CEO, IBM

Meg Whitman—CEO, Hewlett-Packard

Tan Hooi Ling Co-founderr and COO of Grab

Marissa Mayer—CEO, Yahoo

Angela Ahrendts—SVP, Retail, Apple

Padmasree Warrior—Former Chief Technology
and Strategy Officer, Cisco Systems

Getting Certified

I would love to leave you with a few guides on the different certifications in hot demand.

1. Certifications are proof of knowledge—that you are proficient enough to pass the exam.
2. Certifications are not proof of experience—there is no substitute for actually working in the cloud.
3. Certifications are door-openers—they can get you into the interview or the consideration for promotion.

4. Certifications are not golden tickets—they do not ensure a job. They can tee you up for success, but you have to earn it from there.

5. Certifications are not just about earning power.

This is in no way exhaustive but an initial go-to guide for aspiring tech entrants and leaders. I have arranged them by the different certification providers:

FREE GIVEAWAY

There is so much information out there that it can get overwhelming finding your path about which certification to take and when. I have good news!

KINDLY FOLLOW THE URL AND PROVIDE YOUR EMAIL, I WILL SEND YOU AN EXCLUSIVE LIST OF CERTIFICATIONS ARRANGED BY THEIR RESPECTIVE PROVIDER.

REFERENCE SITES

Chapter 1

Lifehack. "7 Ways to Overcome Your Fear of the Unknown And Get More Out of Life," December 27, 2015. https://www.lifehack.org/347868/why-fear-the-unknown.

girlswhocode. "About Us - Girls Who Code." Accessed January 28, 2020. https://girlswhocode.com/about-us/.

"Accenture and Girls Who Code: Closing the Technology Gender Gap." Accessed January 03, 2020. https://www.accenture.com/us-en/blogs/blogs-girls-who-code.

girlswhocode. "Accenture Teams with Girls Who Code to Support Technology Careers for Young Women," November 6, 2014. https://girlswhocode.com/2014/11/06/accenture-teams-with-girls-who-code-to-support-technology-careers-for-young-women/.

Avenue, Human Rights Watch | 350 Fifth, 34th Floor | New York, and NY 10118-3299 USA | t 1.212.290.4700. "Africa: Make Girls' Access to Education a Reality." Human Rights Watch, June 16, 2017. https://www.hrw.org/news/2017/06/16/africa-make-girls-access-education-reality.

"Cracking the Gender Code in Computing | Accenture and Girls Who Code." Accessed April 28, 2020. https://www.accenture.com/us-en/cracking-the-gender-code.

"Culture of Equality in The Workplace | Accenture." Accessed February 09, 2020. https://www.accenture.com/be-en/about/inclusion-diversity/culture-equality-research.

"Frequently Asked Questions | Create My Books." Accessed February 27, 2020. https://www.createmybooks.com/BE/en/faq.

"Gender Equality." Accessed April 28, 2020. https://www.unicef.org/esa/gender-equality.

Sicinski, Adam. "How to Overcome the Fear of Rejection and Regain Your Self-Confidence." *IQ Matrix Blog* (blog), April 22, 2013. https://blog.iqmatrix.com/fear-of-rejection.

Chapter 2

Boss, Jeff. "5 Reasons Why Goal Setting Will Improve Your Focus." Forbes. Accessed April 28, 2020. https://www.forbes.com/sites/jeffboss/2017/01/19/5-reasons-why-goal-setting-will-improve-your-focus/.

"NATIONAL BUREAU OF STATISTICS." Accessed April 28, 2020. https://www.nigerianstat.gov.ng/.

Cynexlink. "Virtual Machines: Pros & Cons," August 18, 2017. https://www.cynexlink.com/2017/08/18/virtual-machines-pros-cons/.

Chapter 3

Develop Good Habits. "13 Steps to Stop Making Excuses and Take Responsibility," May 30, 2018.
https://www.developgoodhabits.com/making-excuses/.

Chapter 4

"Adjusting to a New Environment." Accessed January 15, 2020.
https://www.robertwalters.be/career-advice/adjusting-to-a-new-boss-or-job.html.

Psychology Today. "Familiarity Breeds Enjoyment." Accessed January 28, 2020.
http://www.psychologytoday.com/blog/sapient-nature/201201/familiarity-breeds-enjoyment.

Chapter 5

Eventbrite. "Black Girls CODE Atlanta Chapter Presents: A Day at Accenture Branding!" Accessed March 01, 2020.
https://www.eventbrite.com/e/63985444186?aff=efbneb.

Evensi. "Black Girls CODE Atlanta Chapter Presents: A Day at Accenture Branding! - 2019-07-18 July 2019." Accessed January 14, 2020.
https://www.evensi.com/black-girls-code-atlanta-chapter-presents-day-accenture-branding-75-5th-street-suite-1100/319186339

Chapter 6

Bradford, Full Bio Follow Linkedin Follow Twitter Laurence Bradford wrote about computer programming for The Balance Careers She is a former copywriter turned front-end developer Read The Balance's editorial policies Laurence. "15 of the Most Powerful Women in Tech." The Balance Careers. Accessed March 1 , 2020.
https://www.thebalancecareers.com/powerful-women-in-tech-2071172.

Columbus, Louis. "15 Top Paying IT Certifications In 2019." Forbes. Accessed march 04, 2020. https://www.forbes.com/sites/louiscolumbus/2019/02/11/15-top-paying-it-certifications-in-2019/.

Jain, Neeru. "Top 5 Cloud Certifications in 2018-19 [Updated]." *Whizlabs Blog* (blog), February 16, 2018. https://www.whizlabs.com/blog/5-best-cloud-certifications-in-2018/.

"Oracle Certified Professional (OCP) DBA Salary | PayScale." Accessed January 18, 2020. https://www.payscale.com/research/US/Certification=Oracle_Certified_Professional_(OCP)_DBA/Salary.

Isi Idemudia holds a Ph.D. in Technology Management and works as a Technology Architect Associate Manager at Accenture and lives in Atlanta, Georgia. She has over a decade of experience in technology systems management. She is the mother of two beautiful daughters, Ivana and Shelomi. Because of that, Isi has a passion to see more girls in technology and spends her time coaching girls and young women of all ages.

Though Isi faced several fears while growing up as a girl in Nigeria with no female role models in computer science and technology, and all the odds that she faced in a society that idolizes boys and promotes girl child marriages, Isi faced her fears and rose above these challenges to land a job in a top IT consulting firm.

When Isi moved to the United States, she realized that for her to adequately face her fears in a new environment America, she had to give back to the society and she is doing this by coaching, teaching and motivating young girls to believe in their dreams and helping them overcome their fears about technology being for boys alone. Isi believes in the privilege of learning and more learning to drive out fear. That's why Isi wants girls to know that "girls can code too". Isi, in her efforts to give back, has partnered voluntarily with organizations like Accenture, black girls code, girls who code and the Georgia district 60 to give them the necessary skills they require to thrive in the world of automation. Isi loves to hear from her readers and would love to hear directly from you about this book or any other related subjects. Please email her at: contact@isiai.guru and she will be quick to respond. You can also visit her website isiaiguru.com for more information on the latest information technology certifications and how to pass these exams and validate your skills to the world.

CAN YOU HELP?

Thank You for Reading My Book!

I really appreciate all of your feedback, and I love hearing what you have to say.

I need your input to make the next version of this book and my future books better.

Please leave me an honest review on Amazon, letting me know what you thought of the book.

Thanks so much!

Isi Idemudia (Ph.D.)

Made in the USA
Columbia, SC
22 September 2020